25743-852 7-74 50M ④ OSP

# THE SHIRES

poems by
DONALD DAVIE

Routledge
& Kegan Paul
London

First published in 1974
by Routledge & Kegan Paul Ltd
Broadway House, 68–74 Carter Lane,
London EC4V 5EL
Designed by Andrew Young and Jo Hart
Set in Monophoto Optima
and printed in Great Britain by
BAS Printers Limited, Wallop, Hampshire

ISBN 0 7100 7936 2

# CONTENTS

# ACKNOWLEDGMENTS

The author and publishers wish to thank the editors of *Antaeus*, *The Humanist*, *Meridian*, *The Listener* and *Poetry Nation* for permission to reproduce poems which first appeared in their magazines. Most of the poems were written—in France, Italy and Greece—while I was enjoying a Fellowship granted me by the John Simon Guggenheim Memorial Foundation, for the writing of poems. I am very grateful to the President and the Trustees of the Foundation.

Photographs by Andrew Young illustrate the title page, Bedfordshire, Cambridgeshire, Cheshire, Cornwall, Hampshire, Huntingdonshire, Middlesex, Northamptonshire, Oxfordshire, Suffolk and Worcestershire. The remainder are reproduced by permission of Keystone Press Agency.

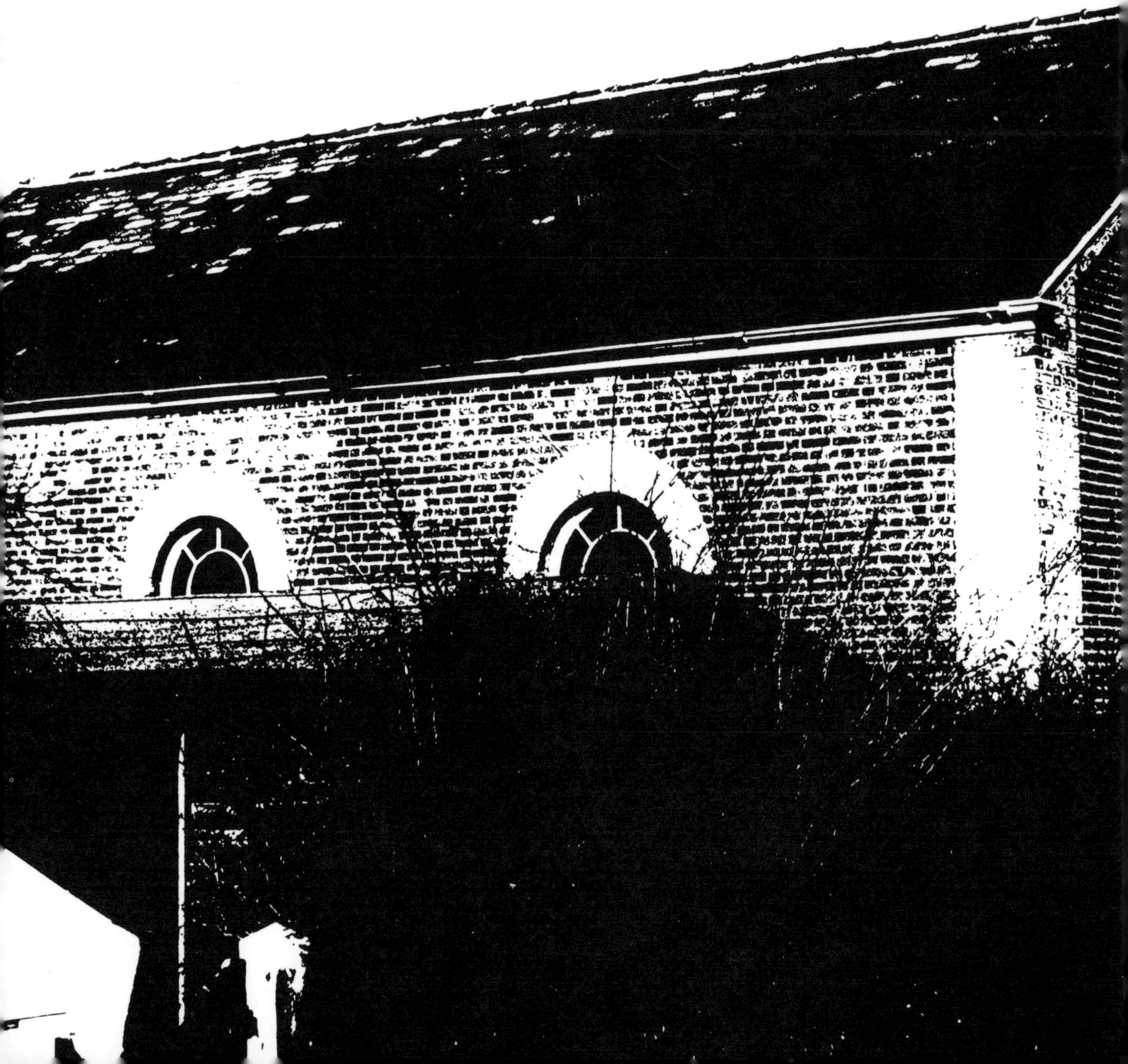

# BEDFORDSHIRE

Bunyan, of course. But Potton it was, or Sandy,
Threaded on the Cambridge road, that showed
Dissenting nineteenth-century demureness
In a brick chapel. I have never known
What to do with this that I am heir to.

My daughter-in-law has studied for her thesis
The Protestant Right in France between the wars,
*l'Association Sully*. Bedfordshire
Might nurse an English counterpart of that:

Our swords for Calvin and the Winter Queen,
The ancient frail collaborating Marshal!

BERKSHIRE
for Michael Hamburger


Don't care for it.
                    We talked of syntax and
synecdoche, the various avant-gardes,
their potencies, their puerilities.
And, Michael, one we knew
in Reading, he approved such conversations;
crippled and dying, he contrived occasions
when they could come about. And yet he
felt (we knew) not scepticism, rather . . .
oh certainly not scepticism, rather
an eager, a too eager warmth in him
starved for a lack of body in that talk.

In his last months I stood him up for supper.
That night I should have stayed with him, I stayed
talking with Christopher Middleton in town.

So nowadays as the biscuit-factory flies
past the train-window and announces Reading,
I keep my head down.

# BUCKINGHAMSHIRE

A thin green salient aimed at the heart of London,
The trains run in and out of Baker Street.

Chalfont St Giles, Chalfont St Peter, Fenny
And Stony Stratford breathe again. The old
A6, the clamorous ditch we edged along,
Ribbons in evening sunlight south to Bletchley.

To west and east the motorways draw off
Poisons that clogged this artery. Abandoned
Transport-cafés blink at the weedy asphalt;
An old white inn by a copse-side yawns and stretches.

## CAMBRIDGESHIRE
'An air that kills' (Housman)


Housman came, savage recluse,
Lover of boys. 'To be sure,
That also I endure,
     yet not from there
Blows into Whewell's Court
     an air that kills.'

Came wincing Gray: 'Why that
Libertine over the way,
Smart of Pembroke, should
     have had the luck
     of running mad
Is more than I can say.'

Smart stares at William Blake:
'Mad? Mad as a refuge
     merely from Locke?
Shame on the subterfuge!
     Let the wind pluck
*Your* wits astray, *then* talk!'

And Blake: 'I accept the reproof.
Better be sane like Housman
Than under Bedlam's roof,
Self-soiled, wind-plucked. And yet
     I think it's not
     an airless place?'

Smart, Gray, all of them, look:
The face of Harold Monro!
'An air that kills? At all
     events, an air!'
Tuneless, he growls from Caius
     in his despair.

# CHESHIRE

A lift to the spirit, when everything fell into place!
So that was what those ruined towers remained from:
Engine-houses, mills. Our Pennine crests
Had not been always mere unfettered space.

Not quite the crests, just under them. The high
Cloughs, I learned in the history-lesson, had
Belted the earliest mills, they had connived
With history then, then history passed them by.

His savage brunt and impetus, one survives it?
Finding it all unchanged and the windowless mill
Between Wincle and Congleton silent and staring, I found
The widow's weeds restorative and fit.

And Mr Auden, whom I never knew,
Is dead in Vienna. A post-industrial landscape
He celebrated often, and expounded
How it can bleakly solace. And that's true.

## CORNWALL
(*Treasure Island*)

Cornwall, the unreality
of Cornwall:

hull-down, the mobile homes
are shelling the Bristol Channel

which fights right back! Storm-lanterns
swing in the black
wind, and tomorrow
perspex and fibre-glass
will slosh about in the eddies.

Cornwall, the fabulous wreckers
of Cornwall: novelists.

A county in Bermuda,
that unreality also.
It was a literary Empire.

Black Jack Pendennis has
been out again. To a lonely
inn upon Bodmin Moor
*etcetera*, on a wild
October night
*etcetera*.

Different for the Cornish,
it must be. But for us
Lancashire and Yorkshire
interlopers who
run curio-shops on the quay
it has, as an arena
for growing old in, one
desolate advantage:
it cannot be believed in.

Black patches on both eyes . . .

## CUMBERLAND

I tend to suppose the part I know least
Of England is the north-west.

A honeymoon in the Lake District
Is conventional matter-of-fact;

And ours was the winter of '45!
On ghyll and yew-tree grove

And packhorse-bridge, the blowtorch air
Was singeing the nostril-hair;

Snow that had lain deep for weeks
Fantasticated our walks;

And Rydal Water to our tread
Rang, till Helvellyn heard.

Exalted by love, in wintry rigours
Unlikely Cumberland rages

Thus in my memories. North-west,
I know you least, or best?

## DERBYSHIRE

We never made it. Time and time again
Sublimity went unexamined when
We turned back home through Winster, lacking heart
For walking further. Yet the Romantic part
Of Via Gellia, where it dives through chasms
To Ashbourne, is historic; there, short spasms
Of horror once in many a heaving breast
Gave Derbyshire a dreadful interest.

And I too was Romantic when I strode
Manfully, aged 12, the upland road.
Only that name of 'Via Gellia' jarred;
It seemed to mean a classical boulevard
With belvederes at intervals. I swelled
My little chest disdainfully, I 'rebelled'!

# DEVONSHIRE

Discharged upon the body of the world
    Drake, Hawkins, all that semen
    Has left no stain! Instead
    The disblitzed Plymouth: first
Violin to squeal the eunuch's part
    Well-planned, a work of art.

We run through a maze of tunnels for our meat
    As rats might; underpass,
    Walkway, crash-barrier lead
    Our willing steps, as does
The questionnaire that we shall be so kind
    As to complete (unsigned)

Between North Road and Paddington. Drake's Circus
    Proffers the hoops the trained
    Corpulent animals are
    Glad to jump through. Drake,
This is the freedom that you sailed from shore
    To save us for?

# DORSET

John Fowles's book, *The French Lieutenant's Woman*:
'A grand ebullient portrait certainly'
Of Thomas Hardy's country, where however
I would not strike such sparkles. Slow and vocal
Amber of a burring baritone
My grandad's voice, not Hardy's, is what stays
Inside me as a slumbrous apogee,
Meridional altitude upon
Pastoral England's longest summer day.

O golden age! Bee-mouth, and honeyed singer!

## COUNTY DURHAM

Driving up from Tees-side
The first and only time,
I had been there before;
I might have been in Goldthorpe.

My cousin kept a shop
For baby-linen in Goldthorpe;
Doing the same in Brighouse
An aunt went out of her mind.

But mostly, visible beauty
Intruded on a coal-field
So little, one was not
Unsettled by its absence.

Coal-field! A term like tundra,
Rain-forest, *karst*, savannah;
A humanly created
Topographical constant.

Indelible! Let rosebay
Willow herb, fiery emblem,
Push as it will, let the pits
Close, there will still be Goldthorpe.

I am told at the miners' gala
They bear green boughs and, Prince-
Bishop, a Lord of Misrule
Preaches in your Cathedral.

And I am supposed to be
Delighted by that survival?
My Lord, your Lord of Misrule
Ruled, and rules, in Goldthorpe.

# ESSEX

Names and things named don't match
Ever. This is not
A plethora of language,
But language's condition;

Sooner or later the whole
Cloth of the language peels off
As wallpaper peels from a wall,
However it 'hangs together'.

With Essex moreover the case is
Especially grievous: hope,
Disappointment, fatuous shocks
And surprises pattern the fabric.

Constable's country merits
Better than I can give it
Who have unfinished business
There, with my own failures.

GLOUCESTERSHIRE
for Charles and Brenda


Not architecture, not
(Good heavens!) city-planning,
But a native gift for townscape
Appears to have distinguished
The pre-industrial English.

Parochialism therefore,
Though of a Tuscan kind,
Discovers in the practice
Of this one homely art
The measure of *civiltà*.

A laudable Little England
Grounded on this conviction
Would fortify the Cotswolds,
Adopting as its tribal
Metropolis Chipping Campden.

# HAMPSHIRE

'Our argute voices vied among the bracken.'
    My sixth-form prize from the North
Was Ronald Bottrall's 'Festivals of Fire',
    My own precocious choice.

A chaste young sailor (One thing I was not
    Precocious at was sex),
Abruptly, two years later, I pronounced
    This verse to a willowy Wren.

An educated girl, she recognized
    The bracken where we stood
Alone together in a woodland ride,
    And took 'argute' on trust.

Past that same wood near Wickham, that same year,
    My nineteenth autumn, I
Rode the country bus from Winchester
    To 'Collingwood' at Fareham.

Alone I'd spent my week-end's leave upon
    St Catherine's Hill, upon
Wolvesey Castle, the Cathedral Close;
    Seen the Round Table, doubtful.

All the South Country that I knew from books!
    Joining the Navy meant
My first time south to London, south from there
    Into my element:

Verses and books, 'argute' and Camelot.
I could correct that Hampshire, but shall not.

## HEREFORDSHIRE

At Hay, or near it, 1944
on winter leave, and walking through the moonlight
the country roads with Gavin Wright, I sealed
with a prompt fear the classical commonplace:
'As one who walks alone at night, and fears
each brigand bush, each clump a nest of spears . . .'
I read that later, out of Juvenal.

A classical region, then? I think so, yes.
Though those were the Welsh Marches, it was not
classical Europe that we beat the bounds of;
barbarians indeed were at our doors
but not round there where, in a world at war,
with atavistic Englishness I saw
the black Black Mountains menacing our acres.

# HERTFORDSHIRE

Was it, I wondered, some freak
of earth or just bad technique
    on the builder's part that made
    the pavement blocks, before
    our friends' house hump and crack?
Could we, as our city shoes slipped,
think Hertfordshire equipped,
    as Kent and Surrey were not,
    thus to resist the encroaching
    concrete apron of London?
No hope of that, alas!
An aspiring middle-class
    could however, we saw,
    make a humanly touching thing
    out of a suburb. It was
not wholly anonymous ground
on which they moved around,
    if it could mutiny thus
    in an Anglo-Jewish enclave
    between Finchley and Barnet.
Displacement and decay
provided for, brought into play
    by a prudent builder ensure
    that, suddenly dying, we leave
    our friends with something to say.

# HUNTINGDONSHIRE

Italian prisoners of war still haunted
    The Huntingdon we quartered
For flats to rent, untimely family
    A student's grant supported.

Many such families, then. The shaking frames
    Of a shared memory feature
A man from Pembroke with his Serbian bride,
    A sexless rawboned creature.

They lived, they said, in a jacked, abandoned bus.
    We wondered: Could they suckle,
Those flattened breasts? And the fingers! Labour Camps
    Had broken every knuckle.

What has become of them? Foolish to ask. But to couples
    We sometimes meet, we assign a
Not dissimilar past: our Roman host
    Has a Polish wife with *angina*.

Huntingdon's bard, androgynous William Cowper,
    Announced it to us all:
That Simoïs and Mincio, like Ouse,
    Sucked down his garden-Wall.

c

# KENT

Chatham was my depot,
Chatty Chatham, 'chatty'
Meaning squalid. So it
Was, the little town
One trundled to out of London
As to a dead-end England.

Of course I knew this was
To get things upside-down;
Still, so it proved for some
Soon after, in E-Boat Alley.

# LANCASHIRE

My father was born in Horton
In Ribblesdale—the highest
Signal-box in England
He'd say, but he was biassed.

Though Horton is in Yorkshire,
The Ribble flows to the west.
I have imagined that river
With awful interest:

Dark gullies, sobbing alders
Must surely mark its course;
It rolls and rounds its boulders
With more than natural force.

For down that sombre valley
(I knew, without being told)
The famous Lancashire witches
Had long ago taken hold,

And a troop of Catholic gentry
Mustered from manors near
Rode hopelessly to Preston
To join the Chevalier.

Liverpool, Manchester, Salford
I've seen, and felt oppressed;
But Clitheroe's haunted river
I've never put to the test.

Should any one taunt me with this,
The sneer's well-merited.
But I pray you, remember my father—
The fault's inherited.

## LEICESTERSHIRE

From a view to a kill in pursuit
Of what can't fill the belly
May do for hunting the fox;
But I. A. Richards on Shelley
Was an obfuscating splendour.

Equally there in Leicester
I listened to the aureate
Archaic tongue of Blunden,
Who through his spell as laureate
Of Oxford smiled and was speechless.

Perhaps the Leicester Poetry
Society is still calling
Its week-end schools together;
It's my fault if I've fallen
Out of touch with its sponsors.

At Loughborough, I remember,
A man too little regarded
(Dead since), V. C. Clinton-
Baddeley afforded
Several views of Yeats.

LINCOLNSHIRE
for Kathleen Wilson


Simpering sideways under a picture-hat
Gainsborough Lady, every Odeon
Or Gaumont of the 'thirties knew her well.

Those British films she regally inclined
To sponsor were, I see now, laying claim
To suavities like Gainsborough the painter's.

Tricked by the name, though, I for years envisaged
Milady at her town in Lincolnshire;
Gainsborough, a sort of Tunbridge Wells.

Beau Nash was there, Beau Brummel took the waters.
If films were shot there (not the ones we saw
Oddly enough), they were demure and tasteful.

The place to go to see the Gainsborough Lady,
As I remember, was the Globe in New Street.
Cousin Kathleen, did you ever go there?

I think you may have done, going or coming
From grandmother's in Day Street. If you did,
Were you, like me, seduced by the genteel?

Easy to see you might be. There were rough
Diamonds all about us; Barnsley-born,
In us some mincing was forgivable.

In Louth that Tory stronghold, in the trilled
Late light on the wolds, a false refinement irks
As not in grimy Gainsborough or Scunthorpe.

# MIDDLESEX

Germans, she said, were sometimes independent;
Her countrymen were all for package-tours,

A girl from Wembley Stadium serving beers
In a Greek bar. A maxiskirt from Bristol
Hawked prints on the Acropolis; from Chepstow
Another served us in a coffee-bar.
Our age-group is dependent, but not theirs.

Temporary drop-outs or true wives
To young and struggling Greeks, they do us more
Credit than we deserve, their timid parents.

The longer loop their Odysseys, the more
Warmly exact the Ithakas they remember:
Thus, home she said was Middlesex, though Wembley
I should have named, indifferently, as 'London'.

MONMOUTHSHIRE
for Doreen


The colonist's 'they' that needs no antecedent;
And as self-evident for the colonized—
Both mouths remorseless. For the Silurist
Self-styled, for Henry Vaughan, both
        Unthinking pronouns missed
The peaceful point three hundred years ago.

Anglo-Welsh: that mixture took and held
Through centuries. My dear wife, we endorsed it:
Our sons are a quarter Welsh if they care to think so.
Our brother-in-law was happy, when the Sappers'
        Reunion was in Chepstow,
To gossip with old comrades of Cawnpore.

# NORFOLK

An arbitrary roll-call
Of worthies: Nelson, Paine,
Vancouver, Robert Walpole.

Vancouver, stolid Dutchman
Born at Lynn, forgotten;
Too much the flogging captain.

Walpole: heaven-high smell of
Whitewash on tainted beef,
Piquant in learning's nostril.

(Unprincipled, vindictive,
All that Pope said, and worse
Confirmed, and spelt as virtue.)

But Nelson and mysterious
Tom Paine, baleful in Thetford,
Napoleonic portents . . .

Who answers for the double
Aspect of genius, arcing
From Corsica or Norfolk?

King's Cliffe, in the evening: that Northampton stone
As fine as Cotswold, and more masculine . . .

Turpin on wheels, my long-lost self that rode
Southward the Great North Road, and had

This bourne in mind, that night was disconcerted:
Youth hostel, yes; also a sort of shrine.

To William Law! Well, later on I learned
To gut that author for my purposes.

Questions remain, however. William Law,
Saint of the English Church . . . And what is sainthood?

Some leading questions must be answered soon,
Lead where they will, scared schoolboy, where they will!

NORTHUMBERLAND
'I hear Aneurin number the dead' (Brigg Flatts)


Johnson's pentameters, nailed by the solid *ictus*;
'Felt percussion of the marching legions.'

Late excavations on the Wall report
The garrisons lived there in their excrement;

Centurions with their centuries, some thousands
—A decimal system drills to a count of ten—
Barked to a halt when Aneurin numbered the dead.

The laboured mole dilapidates, surmounted
By barrel-chests, Aegean or Cymric metres.

# NOTTINGHAMSHIRE

Rosebay willow herb pushing
through patches of old slag
in the curtains of driving rain
obscured the Major Oak.

Or else (our steam was blurring
the windows of the Hillman)
it was our being hounded
out of doors that felled
the last tall stands of Sherwood.

Robin of Locksley, Guy
of Gisborne, and the Sheriff
of Nottingham had been dapples
under my mother's smiles
all down the glades of boyhood.

But now she could take no more
of us, and of our baby.

In the country of *Sons and Lovers*
we think we know all too much
about the love of mothers.

Angry and defiant,
rash on industrial waste,
the rosebay willow herb
is, of all the flowers
she taught me, one I remember.

OXFORDSHIRE

'Start such a fire in England, Master Ridley,
As shall not be put out'—the coupled martyrs
That Oxford steers by in its Morris Minors
Fried for a quibble in Scripture or Canon Law!

Saints we remember, must we remember martyrs?
Baptists though we were, I knew from childhood
Latimer's words, and knew the fire he meant:
Godly work, the pious Reformation.

Crucifixions! Hideousness of burning,
Sizzle of fats, the hideous martyrdoms:
Palach consumed in Prague, a human torch;
A Saigon Buddhist, robe a more lambent saffron;

Dead for a country, dead for a Constitution
(Allende, in his mouth the emptied chamber
Of prompt and fluent deputies). Were these
Crucifixions? They were suicides.

'Martyrs may seek their death, but may not seize it . . .'
Fine scruples, fine distinctions! Can there be
Any too fine for fine-toned Oxford, in
The smell of roast meat and the glare of torches?

## RUTLAND
for George Dekker


Joke county, smallest in England.
But I remember distinctly, more than once,
Swinging the car at the bend by the railway-yards
In Oakham, Rutland's county town. The last
Time was to see—I think you remember, George,
For your own reasons—paintings by my old
Friend, Bill Partridge. Dead now. Had you noticed?

How heavy that weighs, how wide the narrowest shire!

# SHROPSHIRE

This has to be for my school-chum Billy Greaves
Who surfaced out of the past two years ago,
Breaking his journey to Fiji off one of his leaves;
He spoke with me by phone from San Francisco.

If we had met (we agreed upon 'next time'),
Would reminiscences have turned to Clun,
Clungunford, Clunbury, and Housman's rhyme?
('Quietest places,' he called them, 'under the sun.')

Possibly not; though once we wore out brake-blocks
Coasting from Wenlock Edge. And days gone by
Furnish a line of talk that's orthodox
For chance-met class-mates under a foreign sky.

Things change. Gone now the troublesome chores of Empire
That might earn such indulgences. We've seen,
Billy and I, our fractious nation tire
Too soon of holding Suva for the Queen.

Our parents at their tennis-club . . . A high
Lob in the last light hangs like Nemesis
On 1912! Deceived, my father's eye
Foresees the easy smash that he will miss.

Still, I'd quite like it, Billy, if you could
Recall for me above what gravelly flats
In what fly-haunted stream it was, we stood
In the weak light, pyjama-ed, swiping at bats.

## SOMERSET

Antennae of the race,
'the damned and despised *literati* . .

Just how, she wanted to know
(swinging a shopping-bag
from Bridgwater), could
William Pitt have depended
for his intelligence on
a coterie in Racedown:
Coleridge and Southey, Wordsworth?

Big as a mule, a stag
through hedgerows down from Exmoor,
wall-eyed, nostrils flaring,
could not intrude more rudely
upon an *avant-garde*
seminar in the Quantocks.

# STAFFORDSHIRE

The jaunty style of Arnold Bennett's 'Card' . . .

From years ago I call to mind my father,
flushed and uncertain, stalling time after time
a borrowed car in Newcastle-under-Lyme,

who had sung as a young man, 'I was one of the knuts'.

# SUFFOLK

Something gone, something gone out with Nelson,
With him or by him. Something in its place:
A Dynamo! Broke of the Shannon takes,
Crippled in his retirement, a sedate
Pride in totting up the butcher's bills
Of single-ship engagements, finds his own
(His head still singing from an American cutlass)
The bloodiest yet. Audacity of Nelson
Sired Broke and calloused him; Jane Austen hero,
Honourable, monogamous and sober,
Gunnery-expert, servant of the State,
His small estate was somewhere here, in Suffolk.
A better image should be found for it.

My education gave me this bad habit
Of reading history for a hidden plot
And finding it; invariably the same one,
Its fraudulent title always, 'Something Gone'.

Gainsborough might have painted him, with his
Wife and children and a sleek retriever
(Thomas Gainsborough, born at Sudbury)
In a less glaring light, a truer one.

SURREY
'In yonder grave a Druid lies'
(Ode on the Death of Thomson)

Who now reads Thomson or Collins?

'Conifer county of Surrey',
wrote Betjeman, 'approached through
remarkable wrought-iron gates.'

No missing the affection
there, nor the observation.

But on the Thames at Richmond
less tenderly, an eye for
the general more than the pungent
had lifted it to grandeur:

'Suspend the dashing oar.'

SUSSEX

Chiddingly, pronounced
Chiddinglye: the oast-house
Received us with warm brick,
A croquet-lawn, and squirrels.

And like the transatlantic
Visitors we were,
Our self-congratulations
And charmed response were fervent.

The most poeticized
Of English counties, and
An alien poet's eye,
Mine, there to endorse it.

We had to pinch ourselves
To know we knew the rules
Of cricket played on the green.
Our boy will never learn them.

'Brain-drain' one hears no more of,
And that's no loss. There is
Another emigration:
Draining away of love.

WARWICKSHIRE
for Roy Fisher


Eye on the object, eye on the congeries
of objects, eye on the scene
with figures of course, eye on the scene with figures,
delivers us Birmingham. Who is to say it squints?

And yet Spaghetti Junction on the M
6 is, shall we say,
a comparable alternative solution
(to a problem of traffic-flow
in several ways at once on several levels)
to the Piazza d'Aracoeli. Shall we
say that much or in
the Shakespeare country can we? If the tongue
writhes on the foreign syllables, it shows
small relish for your balder registrations,

intent, monocular, faithful.

# WESTMORLAND

Kendal . . . Shap Fell! Is that in Westmorland?
For one who espouses the North,
I am hazy about it, frankly. It's a chosen
North of the mind I take my bearings by,
A stripped style and a wintry;

As on Shap Fell, the only time I was there,
Wind cutting over and snowflakes beginning to sail
Slantwise across, on haulage vans clashing their gears
And me who had walked from Glasgow.

An end-of-October taste, a shade too late
For the right full ripeness. The style is decadent almost,
Emaciated, flayed. One knows such shapes,
Such minds, such people, always in need of a touch
Of frost, not to go pulpy.

# WILTSHIRE

A brutally sheared-off cliff
Walling a cutting between
Barnsley and Doncaster is
The Railway Age in essence.

More cliffs, the hanging gardens
Of gossamer soot as the train
Creeps into Liverpool Street—
This too is in keeping.

But also consider the bugle
And stage-coach clatter silenced;
The beep and vroom of the Daimler
Unheard, and on the chalk

The human beetle rising
And falling for hours in the silence,
The distance: Jude the Obscure
Approaching, on Salisbury Plain.

WORCESTERSHIRE
for D


The best way in (not that I've checked the map)
Might be from West by North, as once we came
After a drive through spooky Radnor Forest
Where you had sat upon a picnic rug
And wept and wept. I laboured into verse
My sense of that, and made no sense at all:

Maria Theresa, I addressed you as,
Imperial sorrow. God knows what I meant
By that, or thought I meant. If I could not
Make you Fair Austria then, I shall not now;
But spin you down, down by whatever stages
Wise maps might tell me, into the blossoming plains.

Feed you with apples, stay you with flagons, Empress!
Acre on acre of orchards of Worcester Pearmains!

## YORKSHIRE
### (Of Graces)

The graces, yes—and the airs! To airs and graces
Equally the West Riding gave no houseroom
When I was young. Ballooning and mincing airs
Put on in the 'down there' of England! I was
Already out of place in the heraldic
Cities of the Midlands—Warwick, Leicester, the South . . .

    —And therefore it is a strain, thinking of Brough
    And Appleby gone from King John to a Frenchman
    For dirty work done on the roads of Poitou.

This helps me—not to pipe like your reed, Bunting,
Master of Northern stops—but to remember,
Never quite well enough, Kirkby Stephen
By Aisgill on to Hawes, to Aysgarth, Askrigg,
The narrow dale past a hump of broken stones.
Slant light out of Lancashire burnished the fell.

Alix, Kate, Eleanor, Anne—Angevin names—
You were not my hopscotch-mates; but Rhoda,
Thelma and Mona. Enormous, their mottled
Fore-arms drove flat-irons later, strove with sheets
In old steam-laundries. There the Saxons queened it
No less—the Elfridas, Enids, many Hildas.

Ladies, ladies! Shirley or Diane or . . .
Which of you girls will be mine? Which of you all
In my dishonourable dreams sits smiling
Alone, at dusk, and knowledgeably sidelong,
Perched on a heap of stones, where 'Dangerous' says
The leaning board, on a green hill south of Brough?

Where is the elf-queen? Where the beldam Belle Dame?
Feyness of the North, kelpie of some small beck
In a swale of marble swirls over Durham,
Irrigates Elmet, combs the peat in Ewden.
And I have no faith in that: *le fay* thinned out
Into a pulse in the grass, St Winifred.

Eleanor rather, Alix, ladies of Latins,
I call you down. (And Mary, Mother of Heaven?)
Justice and Prudence (Prue, a name not given
North of the Trent), Courage, and Temperance were
Your erudite names, mothers of Latin earth.
What *royaume* of earth, elf-queen, did you sway ever?

*Charites* or *Gratiae*, the Graces,
Lemprière says, 'presided over kindness',
Each dam in her own kind fructive. Only two.
(Three came later.) Two: *Hegemone*, the Queen,
And *Auxo*, Increase. Queen of Elfland, in what
Assize did you sit, what increase ever foster?

Now every girl has this elvish admixture.
Thomas of Ercildoune, what you dreamed of once
Fogs every brae-side: lank black the hair hangs down,
The curves of the cheek are hollow and ravaged.
Their womanhood a problematic burden
To them and their castrated mates, they go past.

I have a Grace. Whether or no the Muses
Patronize me, I have a Grace in my house
And no elf-lady. Queen she is called, and Increase,
Though late-come, straitened, of a Northern Province.